Russia

Henry Russell

Laurie Bernstein and Ilya Utekhin, Consultants

NATIONAL GEOGRAPHIC
WASHINGTON, D.C.

Contents

Foreword

Today's Russia is the heir of the Soviet Union, which split into several independent states in 1991. Russia is also the remains of a huge empire that existed before 1917. Although not as big as either the empire or the later union, Russia is still the largest country in the world. It spans 11 time zones across two continents, Europe and Asia, and has coasts on three oceans: the Atlantic, Pacific, and Arctic. Russian territory is unevenly populated and many parts are not suitable for people to live in. The country's territory is a result of a long process of European Russians moving east to settle in new land. Today's Russia is thus a bridge between West and East.

The most significant events in Russian history were attempts to make the country more modern. Three centuries ago, Tsar Peter the Great "opened a window" on Europe when he conquered new lands on the Baltic Sea and undertook economic and cultural reforms. In 1917 a young democracy was swept aside by communist rule, which established itself through war. A huge social experiment began that aimed to create a more equal society. Private property was abolished, religion was banned, and the state distributed everything equally among the citizens. However, people were not free to live as they wished.

For most of the last century, Russia was governed by a non-elected government with policies that cost the lives of many millions of people. They died of starvation or in cruel prison camps. That was the price Russia had to pay to be a superpower equipped with nuclear weapons and home to the largest army in the world. Despite its great achievements in space exploration, the communist system failed to build an efficient economy. In the 1980s Russia finally lost its competition with the Western

world. The Soviet Union was dismantled after the last communist leader, Mikhail Gorbachev, opened the way to reform and democracy.

Russians are proud of their history, especially of the role that the Soviet Union played in the victory over Nazi Germany in World War II. Their country brought to the world some of the greatest writers, musicians, and scientists. Today, Russian citizens hope for a happy and wealthy future, and not without reason: modern Russia has a fast-growing economy and is enjoying an established place among the leading powers of the world.

▲ A wealthy Russian passes a beggar in Moscow. The gap between rich and poor is a major problem facing the Russian people.

Ilya Utekhin
European University of St. Petersburg

The
Greatest
of
Them All

RUSSIA IS THE BIGGEST COUNTRY in the world—it is almost twice the size of Canada, the world's second largest nation. One-tenth of all the land on Earth is Russian territory. From the plains of eastern Europe to the Pacific coast of Asia, Russia stretches across 11 time zones. Its eastern border is only a mile or two from Alaska. From north to south, Russia extends 2,000 miles (3,200 km), almost the width of the United States. Russia's northern edge lies within the Arctic Circle, while parts of its southern border run through the foothills of the Himalaya. Less than one-tenth of Russia is inhabited. Much of the rest is permanently frozen, and there are vast areas in which it is likely that no human being has ever set foot.

◀ **A river empties into the Arctic Ocean in eastern Siberia. For most of the year this remote part of Russia is frozen under a thick layer of snow.**

WHAT'S THE WEATHER LIKE?

Most of Russia has short summers and long winters. Spring and fall pass quickly. The Black Sea coast has a subtropical climate, but the largest part of Russia, Siberia, is colder in winter than any other inhabited part of the world. The map opposite shows the physical features of Russia. Labels on this map and similar maps throughout this book identify most of the places pictured in each chapter.

Fast Facts

OFFICIAL NAME: Russian Federation

FORM OF GOVERNMENT: Federation

CAPITAL: Moscow

POPULATION: 141,377,752

OFFICIAL LANGUAGE: Russian, many minority languages

MONETARY UNIT: Ruble

AREA: 6,592,772 square miles (17,075,200 square kilometers)

BORDERING NATIONS: Azerbaijan, Belarus, China, Estonia, Finland, Georgia, Kazakhstan, Latvia, Lithuania, Mongolia, North Korea, Norway, Poland, Ukraine

HIGHEST POINT: Mount Elbrus 18,510 feet (5,642 meters)

LOWEST POINT: Caspian Sea −92 feet (−28 meters)

MAJOR RIVERS: Amur, Irtysh, Lena, Ob, Volga, Yenisey

Average Temperature & Rainfall

Average High/Low Temperatures; Yearly Rainfall

MURMANSK (NORTHWEST):
55°F (12°C) / 13°F (−10°C); 16 in (41 cm)

MOSCOW (WEST):
61°F (16°C) / 13°F (−10°C); 24 in (60 cm)

IRKUTSK (SOUTH):
64°F (18°C) / −4°F (−20°C); 16 in (41 cm)

VLADIVOSTOK (EAST):
64°F (18°C) / 7°F (−14°C); 28 in (72 cm)

Arctic Ocean

Pacific Ocean

Ural Mountains

S i b e r i a

MAP KEY

Dry
- Arid

Continental
- Cool summer
- Subarctic

Polar
- Tundra

Highland
- Highland

mi

0

km

0   1000

1000

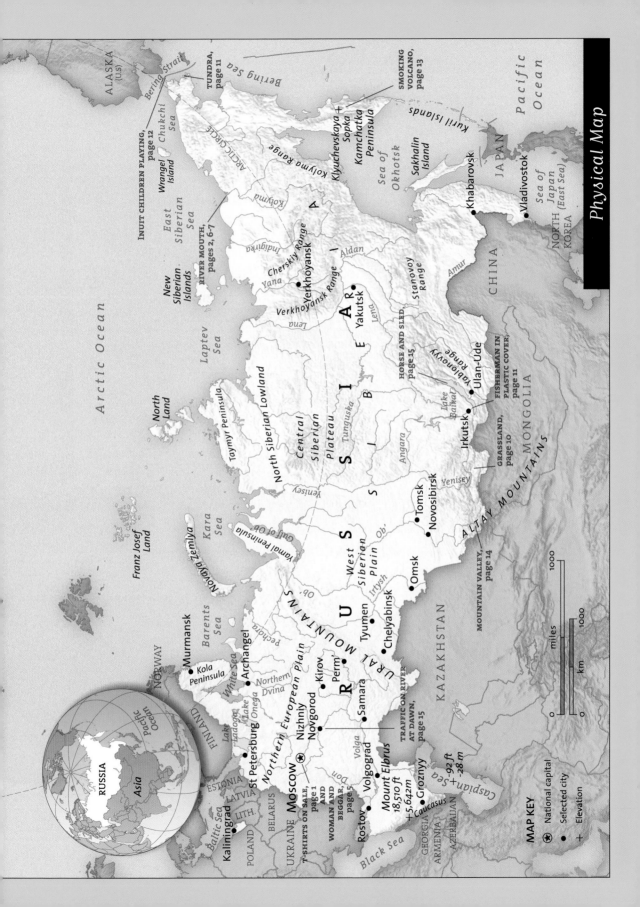

Physical Map

MAP KEY
⊛ National capital
● Selected city
+ Elevation

RUSSIA
Asia
Pacific Ocean

Arctic Ocean
Pacific Ocean
Atlantic Ocean

Callouts / labels:
TUNDRA, page 11
INUIT CHILDREN PLAYING, page 12
SMOKING VOLCANO, page 13
RIVER MOUTH, pages 2, 6–7
HORSE AND SLED, page 15
FISHERMAN IN PLASTIC COVER, page 11
GRASSLAND, page 10
MOUNTAIN VALLEY, page 14
TRAFFIC ON RIVER AT DAWN, page 15
T-SHIRTS ON SALE, page 1 AND WOMAN AND BEGGAR, page 5

Water bodies / oceans:
Arctic Ocean
Pacific Ocean
Bering Strait
Bering Sea
Chukchi Sea
East Siberian Sea
Laptev Sea
Kara Sea
Barents Sea
White Sea
Baltic Sea
Black Sea
Caspian Sea
Sea of Okhotsk
Sea of Japan (East Sea)

Landforms / regions:
ALASKA (US)
Wrangel Island
New Siberian Islands
North Land
Franz Josef Land
Novaya Zemlya
Taymyr Peninsula
Yamal Peninsula
Kola Peninsula
Gulf of Ob
North Siberian Lowland
Central Siberian Plateau
West Siberian Plain
Northern European Plain
URAL MOUNTAINS
ALTAY MOUNTAINS
Cherskiy Range
Verkhoyansk Range
Kolyma Range
Stanovoy Range
Yablonovyy Range
Caucasus
Kamchatka Peninsula
Sakhalin Island
Kuril Islands
SIBERIA
RUSSIA

Rivers / lakes:
Kolyma
Indigirka
Yana
Aldan
Lena
Amur
Tunguska
Angara
Yenisey
Ob
Irtysh
Pechora
Northern Dvina
Volga
Don
Lake Ladoga
Lake Onega
Lake Baikal

Cities:
MOSCOW ⊛
St. Petersburg
Murmansk
Archangel
Kirov
Perm'
Nizhniy Novgorod
Samara
Volgograd
Rostov
Grozniy
Chelyabinsk
Tyumen
Omsk
Novosibirsk
Tomsk
Irkutsk
Ulan-Ude
Yakutsk
Verkhoyansk
Khabarovsk
Vladivostok
Kaliningrad

Elevations:
Mount Elbrus 18,510 ft +5,642m
Caspian Sea −92 ft −28 m
Klyuchevskaya Sopka +

Neighboring countries:
NORWAY
FINLAND
ESTONIA
LATVIA
LITH.
BELARUS
POLAND
UKRAINE
GEORGIA
ARMENIA
AZERBAIJAN
KAZAKHSTAN
MONGOLIA
CHINA
NORTH KOREA
JAPAN

ARCTIC CIRCLE

Scale:
miles 0 1000
km 0 1000

From the Steppes to the Urals

Russia's landscape has a variety of contrasts, from deserts to frozen coastlines and from towering mountains to immense marshes. But in a country this large, the landscapes can cover areas so vast that they seem to be almost endless. If you followed a line on the map between the border with Latvia in the west and the eastern tip of Russia on the Bering Strait, a distance of around 7,000 miles (11,000 km), virtually the whole journey would be across flat plains. Western Russia is mainly steppe. Steppes are great rolling plains without trees. They are similar to the prairies of North America.

The steppes end at the Urals, a 1,560-mile (2,500-km) mountain range that cuts across Russia from north to south. The Urals traditionally mark the border between the continents of Europe and Asia.

▼ Silvery grass stretches across southern Siberia near the Altay Mountains. Grassland, or steppe, like this stretches west in an almost unbroken band until it reaches Ukraine on the western border of Russia.

Into Siberia

The eastern slopes of the Urals mark the start of Siberia. This cold and unwelcoming region takes up just over three-quarters of Russian land. Much of it is composed of conifer forests known as taiga. There are more pines, firs, and other conifers in Russia than in the rest of the world put together. If all of Russia's taiga were joined together, it would cover an area the same size as the entire United States.

Western Siberia is an immense forested plain, which extends to the banks of the Yenisey River. Beyond the river, the land rises into a network of linked mountain ranges that reach their most

▲ This tundra on an island in the Bering Strait east of Siberia is colored by moss and lichens. No trees grow here because it is so cold the soil never thaws out enough for roots to take hold.

ICE-COLD IN SIBERIA

Verkhoyansk is a port on the Yana River with a fur-trading station and a reindeer market. Although the town is wealthy, almost no one wants to live there because it is the coldest town on Earth. The lowest temperature recorded there was −93.6°F (−69.8°C). The January average is −58°F (−50°C). It is so cold that when people breathe out their breath turns to droplets of ice that make a tinkling noise as they hit the ground. When people come in from the cold, they cannot have a hot drink right away—no matter how much they may want one—in case the sudden change of temperature cracks their teeth.

▲ Siberian fishermen dig holes in the ice to fish in frozen rivers. They keep themselves warm with plastic tarpaulins.

spectacular on Kamchatka, the vast volcanic eastern peninsula that extends down into the Pacific Ocean.

A Frozen Ocean

The northern coast of Russia lies on the Arctic Ocean. Almost every mile

▲ Inuit children play on Little Diomede island, part of Alaska. Less than 2 miles (3.2 km) across the frozen sea is Big Diomede Island, part of Russia.

of Russia's north coast is above the Arctic Circle—the only stretches that dip south of the polar region are the White Sea near Archangel and the Gulf of Ob in Siberia. The Northeast Passage, the shipping channel that connects the Atlantic and Pacific oceans across the roof of the world, is frozen for 10 months a year.

The land along the coast and for hundreds of miles inland is permafrost—the ground is frozen so hard that it never thaws completely. Only the upper layer of soil is ice free in the summer. To the south, small plants can grow on the tundra despite the cold temperatures. Around one-tenth of Russia is tundra. Few people live in the far north. Farming is impossible because

THE TUNGUSKA EVENT

Early on the morning of June 30, 1908, a meteorite exploded in midair about 5 miles (8 km) above the Tunguska River Valley in a remote part of Russia, northwest of Lake Baikal. Eyewitnesses saw a blinding flash that seemed to split the sky in two. The meteorite fell apart before it could hit the Earth. Although there is no impact crater, the fireball knocked down 830 square miles (2,150 square km) of forest, and destroyed around 80 million trees. Even a century later, the forest is still thin. Nobody knows how big the meteorite was, but the explosion was 1,000 times greater than the first atomic bomb dropped in 1945.

virtually nothing will grow. There are many valuable minerals in the ground, but mining in the frozen earth is difficult and expensive.

Lonely Islands

Most of Russia's islands are in the Arctic Ocean. The islands are bleak places. If they are inhabited at all, it is usually only by military bases or research stations.

Russia's largest island is Sakhalin, which lies 3 miles (7 km) off the southeastern coast in the Sea of Okhotsk. Sakhalin is 590 miles (950 km) long but as little as 16 miles (25 km) across in places. The island's economy is based on fishing and coal mining. There are also large oil and gas reserves in the area. Life in Sakhalin is difficult because it is so remote. Although the climate is less hostile than in the Arctic, the island is often cold and regularly shrouded in thick fog.

Sunshine Inland

Russia's southern edge crosses more varied landscapes than the north. From the Black Sea coast, it

RED-HOT ON THE PACIFIC

One of the most remote parts of Russia is the eastern peninsula known as Kamchatka. It stretches 780 miles (1,250 km) between the Pacific Ocean and the Sea of Okhotsk. Kamchatka has more volcanoes per square mile than anywhere else in the world. The region has 160 volcanoes altogether, including about 30 that are currently active.

The highest of them is Klyuchevskaya Sopka, which spews out smoke and flames almost constantly. A full-scale eruption in 2007 sent a cloud of smoke 32,000 feet (around 10,000 meters) into the air, disrupting passenger air traffic between Asia and the United States. The ash was carried for thousands of miles on the wind; large quantities of it fell on Alaska.

▼ Smoke pours out of Klyuchevskaya Sopka.

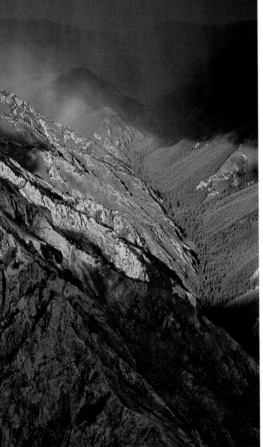

▲ A steep valley cuts into the Altay Mountains, a range that runs along the southern border of Russia.

passes through the Caucasus, a mountain range that contains Russia's highest peak, Mount Elbrus. From there, the frontier runs along the west coast of the Caspian Sea and then across the Central Asian desert on the border with Kazakhstan. To the east, the Russian frontier crosses the Altai Mountains, a range that runs southeast to Mongolia. From there, the border twists around the northeast of China and down to Vladivostok, Russia's eastern port located on a finger of land bound by the Sea of Japan to the east and North Korea to the south.

Water Everywhere

Russia has approximately 100,000 rivers, including some of the longest and most powerful in the world. They are important for transportation and are also major sources of energy. Hydroelectric dams on the rivers generate one-fifth of the nation's energy. The most famous Russian river is the Volga, which rises near Moscow and flows for 2,300 miles (3,700 km) into the Caspian Sea. The Volga is Russia's Mississippi River. Most of the country's population lives within the Volga's vast drainage basin.

The other main rivers lie to the east of the Urals, in Asian Russia. They are generally longer than the Volga. The Ob, Lena, Yenisey, and Amur are in the top ten of the world's longest rivers. However, most of Siberia's

rivers flow north and empty into the Arctic Ocean. As a result, they are frozen near their mouths for most of the year, making them impassable to shipping from the ocean. The rivers are used for transportation in the south, however, and they are also dammed to supply water for farms and cities. A dam on the Ob River near Novosibirsk has created a huge 150-mile (240-km) long reservoir.

Russia also has numerous lakes, including the two largest lakes in Europe—Ladoga and Onega—which lie in the northwest of the country near the Baltic coast. Lake Baikal, in Siberia, is an immense body of water. Although some lakes, such as Lake Superior in North America, cover a larger area, Baikal is so deep that no other lake contains as much water. Lake Baikal contains around one-fifth of all the liquid fresh water in the world.

▲ Like most fresh water in Russia, Lake Baikal freezes in the winter. However, the deep lake is still liquid underneath. Here, an ice fisherman uses a horse and sled to carry his nets.

▼ As dawn breaks, large ships travel past Nizhniy Novgorod, the largest city on the Volga River.

The Biggest of the Big Cats

TIGERS ARE THE LARGEST CATS in the world, and Russia's tigers are the biggest of all. Known as Siberian or Amur tigers, they grow to 10 feet (3 m) long, not counting their tails, and weigh 660 pounds (300 kg). That makes a Siberian tiger four times as heavy as a fully grown man.

Siberian tigers are very rare. In the 1930s, there may have been as few as 50 left in the wild, but their numbers are slowly increasing. In 2005, there were thought to be around 500 Siberian tigers in their forest habitat between the Amur and Ussuri Rivers in the Russian Far East. The rise is thanks to laws that stop hunters from shooting the tigers for their coats, and ban people from killing the tigers' main prey, wild boar and red deer.

◀ A Siberian tiger bares its teeth through the trees. The grimace is not a warning snarl. It is used to sniff deeply, so the tiger can smell prey and rival tigers.

PROTECTING WILDLIFE

In the 19th century, Russian tsars set up national parks across the country. Since that time, Russia has become one of the world's most polluted countries, and its wildlife has suffered. Today, there are 101 protected areas, known as *zapovedniks*, which preserve various habitats—deciduous forest, steppe, taiga, and tundra. The smallest zapovednik covers only 570 acres (2.3 square km); the largest—in the Arctic—covers 1,900 square miles (4,900 square km). Altogether, just over one percent of Russia is given over to zapovedniks. The map opposite shows Russia's vegetation zones—what grows where in the country. Each zone is home to a distinct type of wildlife.

▲ Snow leopards are rare big cats that live in the high mountains of southern Russia.

Species at Risk

Russia is home to some of the world's largest land mammals and many rare and endangered species. The main dangers to their survival are pollution, poaching, and the destruction of their habitats. Government efforts to reduce these threats have had some success, but it is difficult to protect all parts of such a huge country.

Species at risk include:

- Asiatic black bear
- Baikal seal
- Bechstein's bat
- Beluga sturgeon (fish)
- Beluga whale
- Bowhead whale
- Eurasian otter
- European bison
- European mink
- Evorsk vole
- Geoffroy's bat
- Harbor porpoise
- Manchurian zokor (wild goat)
- Mediterranean monk seal
- Northern fur seal
- Polar bear
- Sea otter
- Siberian musk deer
- Siberian tiger
- Snow leopard
- Steller's sea lion
- Steppe pika (rabbit)
- Ussuri tube-nosed bat
- Wolverine
- Wrangel lemming (rodent)

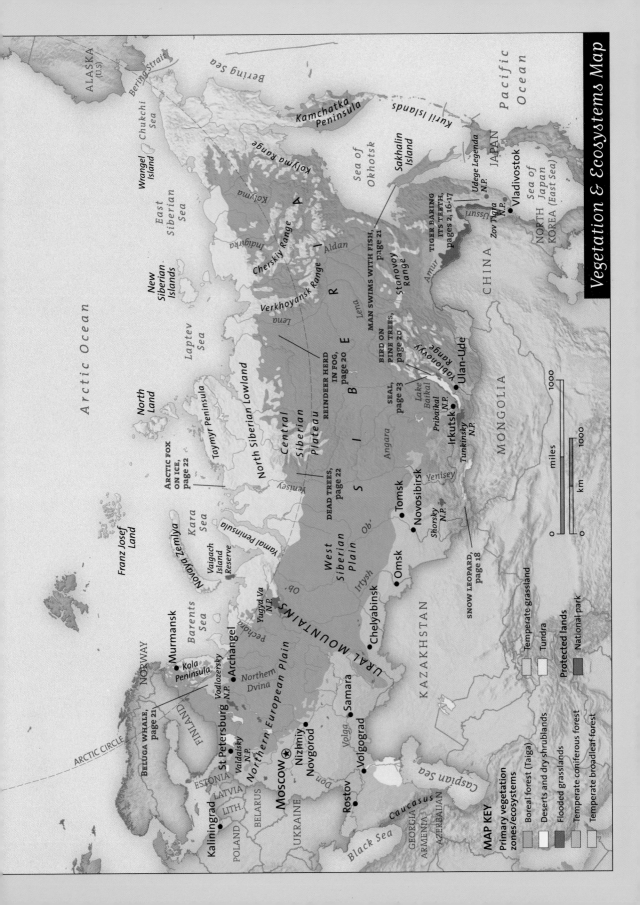

Vegetation & Ecosystems Map

ALASKA (U.S.)

Bering Strait

Bering Sea

Chukchi Sea

Wrangel Island

East Siberian Sea

Kolyma Range

Kolyma

Indigirka

Kamchatka Peninsula

Kuril Islands

JAPAN

Sakhalin Island

Sea of Okhotsk

Pacific Ocean

Udege Legenda N.P.

Vladivostok

Sea of Japan (East Sea)

NORTH KOREA

TIGER BARING ITS TEETH, pages 2, 16–17

Zov Tigra N.P.

Amur

Ussuri

Stanovoy Range

MAN SWIMS WITH FISH, page 21

Cherskiy Range

Aldan

Verkhoyansk Range

Lena

BIRD ON PINE TREES, page 20

Yablonovyy Range

Ulan-Ude

New Siberian Islands

REINDEER HERD IN FOG, page 20

SEAL, page 23

Lake Baikal

Pribaikal N.P.

Irkutsk

Tunkinsky N.P.

MONGOLIA

CHINA

Laptev Sea

North Land

Taymyr Peninsula

Central Siberian Plateau

North Siberian Lowland

Angara

Yenisey

Shorsky N.P.

Novosibirsk

Tomsk

Arctic Ocean

ARCTIC FOX ON ICE, page 22

Yamal Peninsula

Yenisey

DEAD TREES, page 22

West Siberian Plain

Ob

Omsk

Irtysh

SNOW LEOPARD, page 18

KAZAKHSTAN

Franz Josef Land

Kara Sea

Novaya Zemlya

Vaigach Island Reserve

Yugyd Va N.P.

URAL MOUNTAINS

Ob

Chelyabinsk

Barents Sea

Murmansk

Kola Peninsula

Pechora

Archangel

Northern Dvina

Vodlozersky N.P.

Samara

NORWAY

BELUGA WHALE, page 21

ARCTIC CIRCLE

FINLAND

St Petersburg

Valdaisky N.P.

Northern European Plain

Nizhniy Novgorod

Volga

Volgograd

Rostov

Don

Caspian Sea

Caucasus

Black Sea

MOSCOW ✪

ESTONIA

LATVIA

LITH.

Kaliningrad

POLAND

BELARUS

UKRAINE

GEORGIA

ARMENIA

AZERBAIJAN

miles

km

0   1000

0   1000

MAP KEY

Primary vegetation zones/ecosystems

☐ Boreal forest (Taiga)

☐ Deserts and dry shrublands

☐ Flooded grasslands

☐ Temperate coniferous forest

☐ Temperate broadleaf forest

☐ Temperate grassland

☐ Tundra

Protected lands

☐ National park

Span the World

Russia's immense territory stretches almost halfway around the world. As a result, the country contains several vegetation zones, or biomes. A biome is a region that has a particular climate and certain wildlife. Russia's main biomes are tundra (frozen land), steppe (grassland), and taiga (pine forest).

▲ Reindeer spend the summer on the tundra and travel into the taiga forest in the fall.

▼ Most of northern Russia is covered in pine forest.

Cold and Empty

The largest animals on the barren tundra are the reindeer that feed on the mosses and lichens that cling to the icy ground. The reindeer, which are known as caribou in North America, form herds of thousands. Musk oxen, giant hairy relatives of sheep, live in small herds along Siberia's coast.

Lemmings are less visible tundra residents, but they live there in huge numbers. These burrowing, vole-like rodents are the staple diet of two of the region's predators—the arctic fox and the snowy owl.

Huge flocks of ducks, geese, and swans nest in the tundra during its brief summer. They feast on the

WHITE NOISE

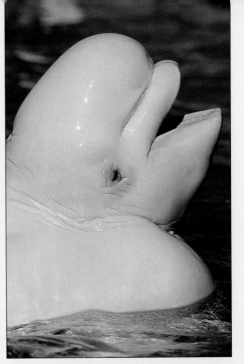

Beluga whales are found not only in Russian waters—they are also common in the cold seas around Alaska and Canada—but they were named by Russians. *Beluga* comes from *bely*, Russian for "white." The whale's pale skin color enables it to hide among floating ice floes while it hunts for fish.

Belugas are small for whales—no more than around 16 feet (5 m) long—but what they lack in size they more than make up in noisiness. They can produce as many as 50 different sounds, including various squawks, whistles, and an amazing bell-like clanging. They are generally agreed to be the chattiest creatures in the sea.

▲ Half of a beluga's body weight is fat that keeps it warm in the icy waters.

insects that swarm across the marshy land. However, when the weather on the tundra turns cold in the fall, the birds fly south for thousands of miles to spend the winter in warmer parts of the world.

Endless Trees

Taiga forest grows in lowland areas of Russia on both sides of the Urals. It also covers the slopes of Russia's mountain ranges. Conifer trees grow well in taiga because they can live for long periods without water. Although the forests are covered in thick snow for several months at a time, there is little liquid water

▼ A man swims in the sea off Sakhalin island. He is not alone in the water. Hundreds of salmon swim around him as they prepare to breed.

for the trees. Taiga trees have waxy needle-shaped leaves, which do not contain much water and so are not damaged by freezing. The trees' sloping, Christmas-tree shape means that snow slides down to the ground and does not weigh down on the branches.

The most common trees along the northern edge of the taiga are larches. Unlike other conifers, these species shed their needles in the fall. This helps them to prepare to survive the Siberian winter.

Bears and Other Animals

Russia is famous for its bears. Polar bears hunt in the Arctic. Brown bears live in the northern taiga, while black bears are found in southern Siberia. The forests are also home to larger animals, such as wild boars and deer. These animals are preyed on by Russia's tiny population of mighty tigers, and smaller animals are hunted by red foxes and lynxes. Small, gray corsac foxes live in eastern Russia.

▲ A forest of larch trees has been stripped of its leaves by pollution from nickel smelters in Siberia.

▼ An arctic fox hunts on the frozen surface of the sea.

Boars and deer are also found on the steppes. However, there are some animals that are found only on the grasslands. For example, many of the steppes have colonies of pikas. These grass-eating relatives of the rabbit are only around 6 inches (15 cm) long. Their coats are so thick and fluffy that the pikas look almost round. Pikas communicate with strange whistling noises. The taiga is also home to many small mammals, such as squirrels and weasel-like sables.

Getting Protection

Pikas and many of Russia's other special animals and landscapes are protected in reserves. Nevertheless, there are still great threats to Russia's wildlife. Global warming is causing the permafrost to melt, which is creating huge, soggy marshes. Polar bears and other Arctic species cannot find enough icy areas to hunt on. Instead they head south to scavenge in towns. The main danger, however, comes from water and air pollution from factories. Russia is upgrading its industry to help keep the environment clean and its wildlife safe.

THE BLUE EYE OF SIBERIA

Lake Baikal contains more water than all of North America's Great Lakes combined. The lake lies east of Irkutsk, with shores 1,492 feet (455 m) above sea level. It is the world's deepest lake—the lowest point is more than one mile (1.6 km) below the surface. Of the 1,000 species of plant and 1,500 species of animal that live in the lake, three-quarters are found nowhere else on Earth. Among them are freshwater sponges and the omul, a relative of the salmon that is caught and eaten smoked by local people.

▼ A Baikal seal, or nerpa, pokes its head out of the lake. This is the only seal species to live in fresh water.

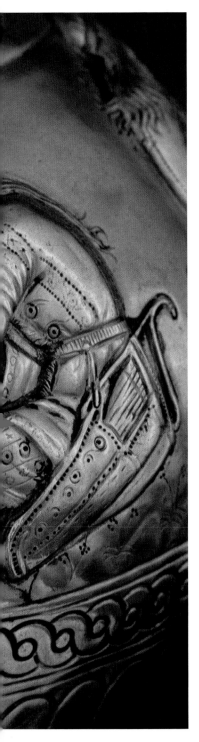

The Road to Russia

I N ITS EARLIEST RECORDED HISTORY, Russia was a route rather than a destination. Over the centuries, waves of Central Asian tribes, such as the Huns, Avars, and Scythians, crossed through Russia on their way to attack Central Europe. These people were nomadic—they had no permanent homes and left few traces of their movements.

Modern Russians are mainly Slavic people originally from what is now Poland, who settled in the Volga River Basin 1,500 years ago. They were joined by Scandinavians known as the Rus. The name *Russia* comes from the Rus people. Together the Rus and Slavs created a system of government from the old tribal system. In A.D. 860 they founded Kiev, the first great city in the region. (Kiev is now in Ukraine.)

◀ This brass pot was dropped in southern Russia by a Scythian horseman 2,500 years ago. It shows a wounded man having his leg bandaged.

ANCIENT CIVILIZATIONS

The first evidence of permanent human settlers in Russia dates from the fifth century A.D., when people from Scandinavia founded villages around the upper section of the Volga River. They later spread south, where they mixed with Slavs who had moved there from the Caucasus Mountains. Together they built a great fortress beside the Dnieper River. That grew into the city of Kiev (now the capital of Ukraine).

Time line

This chart shows the approximate dates of events that have shaped the development of Russia since A.D. 1000

▲ Archaeologists dig down into a kurgan, or burial mound, in the southern part of Asian Russia. The mound is more than 2,000 years old.

Kiev ruled over most of European Russia for the next 200 years. Gradually, however, the territory became too big to control, and it broke up into three main regions. One of these would later become Ukraine in the south; another was Belarus (White Russia) in the west; the third was Muscovy in the northeast. Muscovy eventually gave birth to modern Russia.

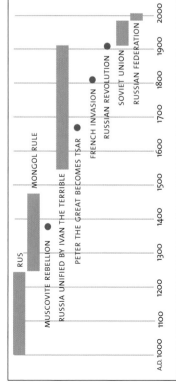

RUS

MUSCOVITE REBELLION

MONGOL RULE

RUSSIA UNIFIED BY IVAN THE TERRIBLE

PETER THE GREAT BECOMES TSAR

FRENCH INVASION

RUSSIAN REVOLUTION

SOVIET UNION

RUSSIAN FEDERATION

A.D. 1000   1100   1200   1300   1400   1500   1600   1700   1800   1900   2000

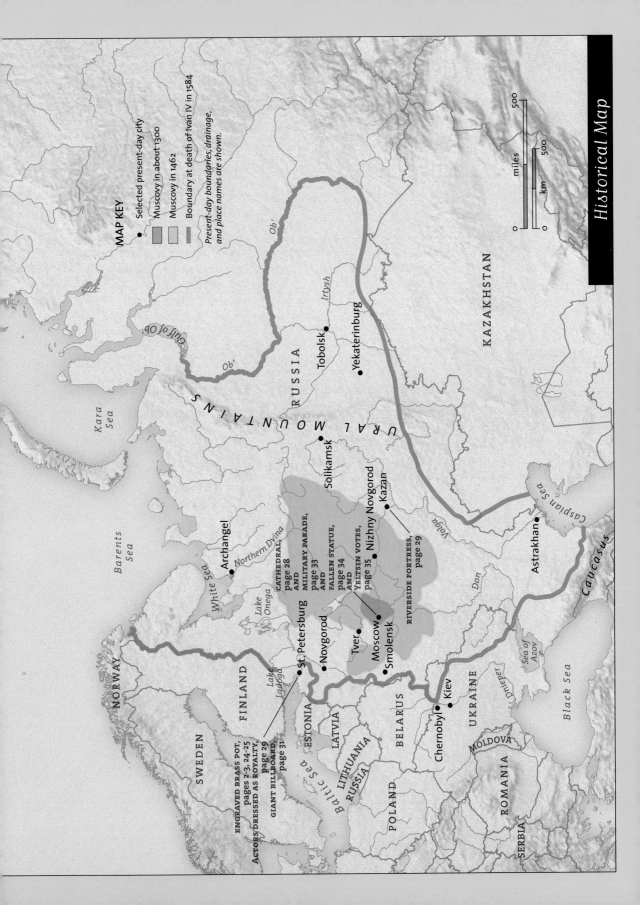

Historical Map

MAP KEY

• Selected present-day city

Muscovy in about 1300

Muscovy in 1462

Boundary at death of Ivan IV in 1584

*Present-day boundaries, drainage,
and place names are shown.*

0   500   miles
0   500   km

NORWAY

SWEDEN

FINLAND

Barents Sea

Kara Sea

Gulf of Ob'

Ob'

Ob'

Irtysh

Tobolsk

• Yekaterinburg

KAZAKHSTAN

RUSSIA

U R A L   M O U N T A I N S

White Sea

Lake Onega

Lake Ladoga

• Archangel

Northern Dvina

Solikamsk

Nizhny Novgorod

Kazan

St. Petersburg

• Novgorod

Tver

Moscow

Smolensk

Volga

Don

Astrakhan

Caspian Sea

Caucasus

ESTONIA

LATVIA

LITHUANIA

RUSSIA

Baltic Sea

POLAND

BELARUS

UKRAINE

MOLDOVA

ROMANIA

SERBIA

Chernobyl

• Kiev

Dnieper

Sea of Azov

Black Sea

ENGRAVED BRASS POT,
Pages 2–3, 24–25, AND
ACTORS DRESSED AS ROYALTY,
page 29 AND
GIANT BILLBOARD,
page 31

CATHEDRAL,
page 28 AND
MILITARY PARADE,
page 33 AND
FALLEN STATUE,
page 34 AND
YELTSIN VOTES,
page 35 AND
RIVERSIDE FORTRESS,
page 29

Moscow and Muscovy

Until the 13th century, Moscow, the capital of the state of Muscovy, was a small trading post among the cold northern forests. Most people lived farther south, near Kiev. That was where Mongol invaders from Asia headed in the 1240s. The Mongols soon crushed southern Russia, adding it to their huge empire.

Apart from a few raids, the Mongols left Muscovy largely alone. In southern Russia, the Mongols were cruel rulers, and people headed to Moscow to live in safety. Over the years, Moscow grew into the main Russian city and became a center of resistance against the Mongols. In 1480, the Muscovites managed to drive the Mongols out of northern Russia. The Mongols continued to control southeastern Russia until the 1550s, when the whole area was united under the Muscovite ruler Ivan IV. Ivan became the first tsar.

▼ St. Basil's Cathedral in central Moscow is one of the most famous buildings in Russia. It was built by Russia's first emperor, Ivan IV, in 1561.

WHAT'S SO TERRIBLE ABOUT IVAN?

Ivan IV, Russia's first tsar, is known by the nickname Ivan the Terrible—but it does not mean quite what it seems. Ivan's nickname in Russian is *grozny*, which means "awesome" rather than "terrible." The name actually celebrates Ivan's remarkable achievement of uniting Russia. Ivan does have a reputation for cruelty—but it may be undeserved. He was said to have killed his own son, for example, but historians now think that this was probably an accident. One of Ivan's successors, Peter the Great, went one step further. He had his son deliberately tortured to death!

▲ A fortress stands beside the Volga River in Kazan, southern Russia. Ivan the Terrible took control of this city from the Mongols in 1552.

A Grand Nation

Russia grew into a powerful country and expanded to the east. By 1648, Russians lived on the Bering Strait on the eastern tip of Asia. Russian settlers later crossed the strait and set up communities in what is now the U.S. state of Alaska.

Peter the Great became tsar in 1682. He transformed Russia into a modern empire. He moved his capital from Moscow to St. Petersburg, a new city built on the Baltic coast to the tsar's own design.

Life was good for Russian nobles but incredibly tough for the poorest people. They were the serfs, who were the property of wealthy landowners, perhaps the tsar himself or even parts of the powerful Russian Church. People

▼ Actors dressed as Peter the Great and his wife Catherine. Their rule marked a golden age for Russia.

were born into serfdom and spent their whole lives working for their owners, usually as agricultural laborers.

Seeds of Revolt

Serfdom had once existed in many countries, but by the 19th century most European countries had ended the practice. At that time, however, half of all Russians were serfs, totalling 20 million people.

In the 1850s, Tzar Alexander II realized that an economy based on serfdom could not compete with the industrial strength of other European countries. Alexander decided to emancipate, or free, all serfs. He persuaded objectors by saying, "It is better to abolish serfdom from above, than to wait for the time when it will abolish itself from below." In 1861, serfdom came to an end. Many former serfs moved to Russia's growing cities to find work in industry. However, the divide between rich and poor remained as large as

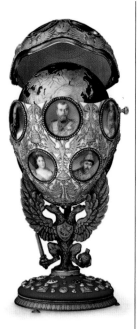

▲ A decoration made by the jeweler Fabergé displays portraits of the Romanovs, Russia's royal family.

I'M ANASTASIA!

In the few months after the Russian Revolution, Tsar Nicholas II, his wife, and their five children were held prisoner on the orders of the Lenin. In July 1918, they were shot dead at a remote house. Until recently, no one knew what had really happened, and there were rumors that the tsar's daughter, 17-year-old Anastasia, had escaped alive. Several women later claimed to be the Russian duchess. Many of them wanted the vast sums of money stashed away in the royal family's

▲ Anna Anderson claimed to be Anastasia and was buried under the name—but her claim was false.

Swiss bank accounts. In 1991, the claimants were proven to be con artists. The remains of the royal family—including Anastasia—were found buried close to where they had died.

ever. Resentment against the ruling class continued to grow. Alexander II himself was assassinated by revolutionaries who blew him up in 1881.

Time for Revolution

At the start of the 20th century, the tsarist government was less popular than ever. Revolutionary groups argued that the tsar should be overthrown and a fairer system put in place. In 1914, Russia was drawn into World War I, fighting on the side of Britain, France, and later the United States against Germany and Austria-Hungary. The Russian economy could not feed its soldiers or make weapons for them.

▲ People are dwarfed by a giant picture of Lenin, who made Russia the first communist country in 1917.

In the spring of 1917, workers and soldiers rebelled. The tsar abdicated, or left office, and the people elected a government. The new leaders struggled to establish control. A few months later the Bolsheviks, a small group of communists led by Vladimir Lenin, seized power in a violent revolution. The communist Red Army defeated anticommunist forces in a bloody civil war that lasted almost three years and left Lenin in control of the country.

Lenin set up the Union of Soviet Socialist Republics (the USSR or Soviet Union). Russia was the largest and most important of the 12 republics that belonged to the union. Moscow became the national capital again.

When Lenin died in 1924, Russia's new leader, Joseph Stalin, tried to industrialize Russia, but his methods were brutal. Tens of millions of people starved when Stalin's plans for agriculture failed to produce enough food. Others were executed for opposing him. Millions more were sent to prison camps in Siberia, where many died.

The Worst War Ever

In the early years of World War II (1939–1945), the Soviets invaded the Baltic states. Estonia, Latvia, and Lithuania became part of the USSR. Stalin had agreed to share territory in eastern Europe with Nazi Germany. However, in 1941 the German leader Adolf Hitler turned on his ally and invaded the Soviet Union. German troops reached Moscow, but were driven back by the Red Army. Losses were huge on both

SENT TO SIBERIA

The rulers of Russia had long sent their political opponents to Siberia, far from the centers of power. The communist rulers sent more people there than ever before. Stalin created a network of prisons known as the Gulag, which in Russian is short for Chief Administration for Corrective Labor Camps. Millions of people died in the Gulag.

Alexander Solzhenitsyn, an author who was imprisoned in Siberia, wrote about his own experiences in books, such as *The Gulag Archipelago* (1968). This book was banned in Russia. The manuscript was smuggled out of

▲ The gate of a notorious Siberian camp where prisoners mined uranium for nuclear bombs

the country and published in English in 1973. Although some illegal copies were smuggled into the country, *The Gulag Archipelago* was not officially published in Russia until 1989.

sides. The Soviet Union lost 9 million soldiers and 18 million civilians. Russia remembers the conflict as The Great Patriotic War.

Colder Times

At the end of the war, the Soviet Union was left in control of much of eastern Europe. It set up communist governments in East Germany, Bulgaria, Hungary, Poland, Romania, and Czechoslovakia. The western border of those countries formed the so-called "iron curtain" across Europe.

In 1949 the Soviet Union announced that it had started making atomic bombs. The announcement was part of the Cold War, a 40-year stand-off between the Soviets and their allies and the world's other superpower, the United States, and its allies. Both sides competed for global dominance. In 1962, the Soviets stationed missiles in Cuba. The world was poised on the brink of nuclear war until the Soviet leaders agreed to remove the weapons in return for U.S. missiles leaving Turkey.

▲ A parade of rocket-launchers drives through Moscow's Red Square past the Kremlin during the annual May Day celebrations. Each May Day the communist Red Army showed off its strength to Russia's rulers and the country's Cold War enemies.

Under Pressure

The Soviet Union found it difficult to keep up with its more wealthy rival. It could not afford the Americans' missile production and huge army. In the 1950s and

1960s, both countries also plowed money into the costly "Space Race."

A war in Afghanistan in the 1980s put even more pressure on the Soviet economy. The country began to collapse. In 1986 an explosion at a nuclear plant in Chernobyl, Ukraine, released a radioactive cloud so large that it could be seen from space. The Soviets could no longer hide their problems.

▲ A statue of Stalin lies toppled in a Moscow park after the fall of Russia's communist government in 1991.

SUCCESS IN SPACE

Although the United States was the first nation to put a man on the moon in 1969, the early part of the space race was led by the Soviet Union. The first artificial satellite to orbit the Earth was the Soviet Sputnik I in 1957. The first man in space was Yuri Gagarin, a Russian from Smolensk, in 1961. The first person to walk in space was Alexei Leonov, from Irkutsk, in 1965. Two years after U.S. astronaut Neil Armstrong took his moon walk, the Soviet Union launched the world's first space station, Salyut I.

◀ Tourists visit a replica of the Vostock rocket that launched Yuri Gagarin into orbit in 1961.

So Long, Soviets

The Soviet leader, Mikhail Gorbachev, tried to modernize the country, although he meant it to stay communist. He remained in control of the Soviet Union, but he allowed Russia and the other republics to hold elections. In June 1991, Boris Yeltsin won the first free election since 1917, and became president of Russia.

Russian communists tried to seize power in August 1991. They failed, but their attempted coup weakened Gorbachev, who could no

GLASNOST AND PERESTROIKA

In 1985, when Mikhail Gorbachev came to power in the Soviet Union, the country was broke. The new leader announced: "Life cannot be lived like this any longer." He introduced two new policies: *Glasnost* (openness) and *Perestroika* (reconstruction). The policies allowed Russians to discuss politics for the first time. That paved the way for the end of communism after 74 years. Gorbachev also helped to end the Cold War by agreeing with U.S. leader Ronald Reagan to reduce the number of nuclear weapons each country aimed at the other.

▲ Mikhail Gorbachev (*right*) with U.S. President Ronald Reagan during a meeting in 1987.

longer hold the Soviet Union together. It broke apart. Russia was once more a separate country—known as the Russian Federation—and a democracy.

Pain and Change

The economy began a painful change from a system run by the government to a free market. The poor became poorer, and the state no longer supported them. To raise cash, the government sold off state industries.

Yeltsin resigned in 1999 and was succeeded by Vladimir Putin, who won elections in 2000 and 2004. Putin continued economic reforms, but was criticized for his treatment of political opponents, particularly in the Caucasus, where peoples such as the Chechens wanted independence from Russia.

▼ Boris Yeltsin casts his vote in 1991, during Russia's first democratic election in 74 years.

Many Peoples, One Russia

EIGHTY PERCENT OF RUSSIANS belong to an ethnic group called the East Slavs. They are the descendants of the people who settled in the area about 1,500 years ago. Tatars, who arrived several centuries ago with Mongol invaders, are the next largest group. They make up about 4 percent of the population. The third largest group is Ukrainian (2 percent). Although Ukraine is now an independent country, there has always been a lot of mixing between the two nations: 17 percent of Ukrainian citizens are originally from Russia.

All but a few citizens speak Russian, but several dozen other languages are also used, including Tatar in the Caucasus Mountains and several Siberian languages, such as Komi and Yakut.

◄ Russians celebrate the arrival of democracy in Kaliningrad, a port on the Baltic Sea. The city is a small patch of Russia that is surrounded by Poland and Lithuania.

TO THE CITY

Three out of four Russians live in cities. The two largest are Moscow (10.5 million) and St. Petersburg (4.6 million). Eleven other cities have more than a million people. The countryside is a very different story. Woodland areas have just 250 people living per square mile (100 per square km), while that figure drops to almost zero in the tundra regions of the north.

▲ Many Russian cities are very remote. Petropavlosk, the capital of Kamchatka, is 4,200 miles (6,759 km) away from Moscow.

1950 / 103 million	1970 / 130 million	1990 / 148 million	2005 / 143 million
45% urban · 55% rural	63% urban · 37% rural	73% urban · 27% rural	73% urban · 27% rural

Common Russian Phrases

There are about 120 ethnic groups in Russia and they speak more than 100 languages. All but a few remote Siberian communities can speak Russian.

Hello	Zdravtsvuitye (ZDRAST-vweet-yeh)
Goodbye	Do svidanya (dah svi-DAHN-yuh)
Yes	Da (DAH)
No	Nyet
Please	Pozhaluistye (Pa-ZHAL-ist-yeh)
Thank you	Spasibo (spa-SEE-buh)
My name is...	Menya zavut... (men-YA za-voot...)
How are you?	Kak dela? (Kack dyel-AH)
I don't speak Russian	Ya ne govoryu po russki (yah nyeh gah-vah-roo pah ROOS-ki)
Do you speak English?	Govoritye po angliski? (gah-vah-REET-yeh pah ahn-GLEES-ki)

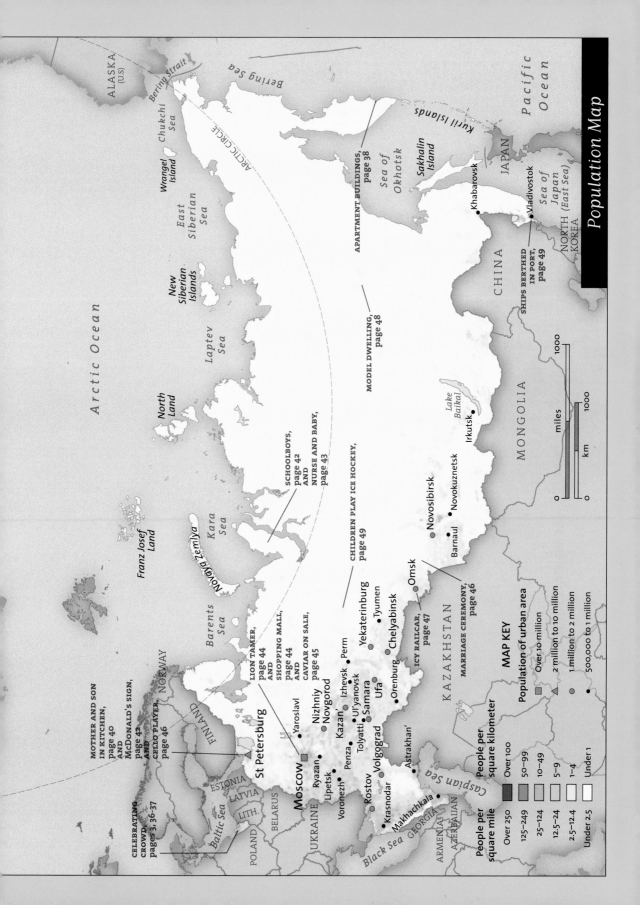

Population Map

MAP KEY

People per square kilometer
- Over 100
- 50–99
- 10–49
- 5–9
- 1–4
- Under 1

People per square mile
- Over 250
- 125–249
- 25–124
- 12.5–24
- 2.5–12.4
- Under 2.5

Population of urban area
- ■ Over 10 million
- ▲ 2 million to 10 million
- ● 1 million to 2 million
- ● 500,000 to 1 million

CELEBRATING CROWD, pages 3, 36–37

MOTHER AND SON IN KITCHEN, page 40 AND **McDONALD'S SIGN,** page 42 AND **CELLO PLAYER,** page 46

LION TAMER, page 44 AND **SHOPPING MALL,** page 44 AND **CAVIAR ON SALE,** page 45

SCHOOLBOYS, page 42 AND **NURSE AND BABY,** page 43

CHILDREN PLAY ICE HOCKEY, page 49

MODEL DWELLING, page 48

APARTMENT BUILDINGS, page 38

ICY RAILCAR, page 47

MARRIAGE CEREMONY, page 46

SHIPS BERTHED IN PORT, page 49

ALASKA (US)

Bering Strait

Bering Sea

Chukchi Sea

Arctic Ocean

ARCTIC CIRCLE

Wrangel Island

East Siberian Sea

New Siberian Islands

Laptev Sea

North Land

Franz Josef Land

Novaya Zemlya

Kara Sea

Barents Sea

NORWAY

FINLAND

St Petersburg

Yaroslavl

Moscow

Ryazan'

Lipetsk

Voronezh

Nizhniy Novgorod

Izhevsk

Kazan'

Perm

Ul'yanovsk

Penza

Tolyatti

Samara

Ufa

Rostov

Volgograd

Orenburg

Krasnodar

Astrakhan'

Makhachkala

Yekaterinburg

Tyumen

Chelyabinsk

Omsk

Novosibirsk

Novokuznetsk

Barnaul

Irkutsk

Lake Baikal

KAZAKHSTAN

MONGOLIA

CHINA

Khabarovsk

Vladivostok

Sea of Japan (East Sea)

JAPAN

NORTH KOREA

Sea of Okhotsk

Sakhalin Island

Kuril Islands

Pacific Ocean

ESTONIA

LATVIA

LITH.

BELARUS

POLAND

UKRAINE

Baltic Sea

Black Sea

Caspian Sea

GEORGIA

ARMENIA

AZERBAIJAN

miles

km

0   1000

0   1000

At Home and On Vacation

Most Russians live in apartments in towns and cities. Under communism, it was illegal for a private individual to own land in towns and cities. However, today more than half of all homes belong to the people who live in them. A Russian family apartment is often much smaller than a similar home in a U.S. city or in western Europe. Partly as a result, Russian families tend to be small: It is unusual for a married couple to have more than two children. Both parents go to work because that is the tradition and because they need two incomes to live comfortably.

▼ A mother and son prepare a meal in the kitchen of a small apartment in St. Petersburg, Russia's second-largest city.

In rural areas, many people still live and work on the collective farms that were set up all over the country when it was part of the Soviet Union. Today the farms are owned by several families or are run by a company.

Wealthier Russians have two homes, one in the city and a holiday cabin, or dacha, in the countryside. The most valuable dachas are at top vacation resorts on the Black Sea coast.

It's All Russian

Russians must go to school from the age of six or seven. However, because most families have two working parents and need someone to look after their children, education often begins much earlier. More than three-quarters of Russian children go to preschool between the ages of three and six.

All students learn Russian, although in areas where another language is common, lessons are sometimes also held in that language. At 15 or 16, all Russian pupils take a basic general education test. Some then get jobs, but most students continue in school for another two years to study for their secondary education diploma. Lessons at this level and all college courses are always taught in Russian.

NATIONAL HOLIDAYS

Some of Russia's holidays are Christian festivals. However, they are celebrated on different dates from other countries because the Russian Church follows its own calendar. For example, in Russia Christmas is celebrated after New Year.

Other national days commemorate Russia's military history. February 23 honors the members of the armed forces. May 9 celebrates the victory over the Nazis in 1945.

June 12 is the anniversary of the day in 1990 when modern Russia was created and the Soviet Union was dismantled. A holiday in November once marked the anniversary of the 1917 revolution. Russians still take a day off, but today the holiday officially honors a victory in a war with Poland in the 17th century.

JANUARY 1–5	New Year
JANUARY 7	Christmas Day
FEBRUARY 23	Protector of the Fatherland Day
MARCH 8	International Women's Day
MAY 1	Labor Day
MAY 9	Victory Day
JUNE 12	Day of Russia
NOVEMBER 4	Day of National Unity

Nenets from the Arctic of western Russia speak their own language. They must learn Russian at school.

It is hard to get into college in Russia. There are many more applicants than places, and only the best students make it. In most subjects, it takes five years to get a degree. Under the Soviet system, all education was free and controlled by the government.

THE RUSSIAN ALPHABET

The Russian alphabet has 33 letters—seven more than the alphabet used to write English. The letters A, K, M, O, and T are the same in both languages. Other Russian characters look the same as Western letters but have different sounds. The English equivalents of the Russian B, H, P, and C are V, N, R, and S, respectively. Many Russian letters are also based on characters from Greek, which was spoken by the monks who first brought the Bible and other books to the Slavs in the 9th century. One of the most famous missionaries was St. Cyril, who was said to have invented the Russian way of writing. The story is probably not true, but the script is named Cyrillic in his honor.

The sign of a famous burger chain is easy to read, even in Russian.

Since the fall of communism in 1991, hundreds of privately funded schools and colleges have opened in many parts of the country.

Bad Health

The Russian health-care system is paid for by the government, yet few hospitals have modern facilities or the latest medical equipment. Doctors and nurses struggle to cope with the demands placed on them by the large number of people who eat very poor diets. Russia also has serious health problems caused by alcoholism, smoking, and environmental pollution. The population is falling: Every year, more Russians die than are born. Life expectancy is 73 years for women and only 59 years for men. (In the United States, the equivalents are 80 for women and 75 for men.)

▼ A Russian nurse holds up a newborn baby at a Russian children's hospital. Russian medical staff traditionally wear hats that look like those worn by chefs in other countries.

Cabbage and Beets

In modern Russia, food has an international flavor—dishes may come from all over the world. Traditional Russian food is wholesome but rather plain. Warm stews of meat, fish, poultry, or game are among the common dishes. For cold days, there is a wide variety of hot soups, including *shchi*, which is made of cabbage, the nation's most commonly used vegetable. A typical cold soup for the summer months is *okroshka*.

▲ Shoppers walk through the galleries of GUM, Moscow's largest food hall and department store.

The ingredients of okroshka can vary—it may contain cold meat or fish—but the liquid part is always *kvass*. Kvass is a fizzy drink made from bread.

Among the most famous Russian dishes are borscht—a beet soup that may be served hot or cold—and *blinis*, thin wheat pancakes that can be

MOSCOW STATE CIRCUS

The Moscow State Circus is one of the most famous circuses in the world. It was founded in the 18th century. Since then, its acrobats have amazed audiences with their contortions and death-defying trapeze acts. Nationalized after the Russian Revolution in 1917, for the next 74 years the circus undertook regular tours throughout the Soviet Union: It visited most major cities five or six times a year. Since the fall of communism in 1991, the Moscow State Circus has cast its net more widely. It now goes on regular international tours, and every performance is a sellout.

▲ A lion walks along tightropes under the watchful eye of a trainer.

wrapped around almost anything, savory or sweet. A special delicacy is caviar, the roe or eggs of the sturgeon. These fish are common in the Volga River, but the best caviar comes from the beluga sturgeon of the Caspian Sea. Because this is an endangered species, the amount of this type of caviar that can be produced each year is strictly limited.

Russians also drink a lot of tea served without milk in a glass. Today, people brew their tea with electric kettles, but traditionally Russian tea is brewed with water from a coal-fired metal urn known as a samovar.

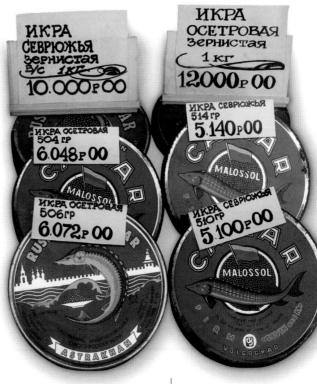

▲ Tins of caviar are on sale in a Moscow store. Beluga caviar is one of the world's most expensive delicacies. It is priced at about $225 per pound.

World Class

Many of the world's greatest writers and musicians have been Russians. The nation's best-loved author is the poet and playwright Alexander Pushkin. Other famous names include the 19th-century novelists Leo Tolstoy, author of *War and Peace*, and Fyodor Dostoyevsky, whose works include *Crime and Punishment*. Another major writer of that period is Anton Chekhov, a doctor who became a playwright. The leading writers of the 20th century were Boris Pasternak, author of *Doctor Zhivago*, and Alexander

▲ A Russian cellist practices in his apartment. There is a strong tradition of string music in Russia.

▼ Two couples are married in a joint ceremony at a Russian Orthodox church. Brides and grooms traditionally wear crowns.

Solzhenitsyn, whose accounts of life in Russia brought home the truth about communism.

There are many outstanding Russian composers as well. Pyotr Ilyich Tchaikovsky created the famous ballets *The Nutcracker Suite* and *Swan Lake*. Sergei Prokofiev wrote the music for the story *Peter and the Wolf*, which uses a different melody for each character.

Famous Movies and Dancers

Russian film directors have also made their mark. Sergei Eisenstein's film *Battleship Potemkin* in 1925 tells a story from a military rebellion in 1905. That film has influenced many other movies, including the Oscar-winning Mafia story *The Untouchables*, which was made over 60 years later. Andrei Tarkovsky's 1972 science-fiction classic *Solaris* was remade in 2002 starring the Hollywood actor George Clooney.

Russia is also renowned for its ballet. It has two outstanding companies: the Bolshoi (meaning "big") and the Mariinsky (once known as the Kirov). A long line of acclaimed

EAST MEETS WEST

The Trans-Siberian railroad is the main surface link between Moscow and the Russian Far East. The express passenger train that connects the capital with Vladivostok takes just over a week—seven days, five hours, and 45 minutes—to complete the 5,778-mile (9,198-km) journey.

The railroad took 25 years to complete. By 1916 the track was ready for trains to travel east from Moscow's Yaroslavl Station. The railroad passes through most of Russia's large regional centers, such as Nizhni Novgorod, Perm, Yekaterinburg, Omsk, Novosibirsk, and Irkutsk. A branch-line splits off near Irkutsk, crosses Mongolia, and goes as far a Beijing, China.

▲ The Trans-Siberian railroad travels through the southern part of Russia.

▶ Children look through the frosted window of a carriage on the Trans-Siberian railroad.

Russian dancers include Vaslav Nijinksy, Rudolf Nureyev, and Natalia Makarova.

Orthodox Religion

The main religion in Russia is Russian Orthodoxy, which was established in A.D. 988. It is a form of Christianity based on the practices of the Eastern Church of Constantinople (the modern city of Istanbul, Turkey). About 60 percent of Russians describe themselves as Russian Orthodox Christians. Far fewer go to church, however. That may be because many people still

SAKHA

Many of Russia's ethnic groups are Turkic peoples. Most of them live in the Caucasus Mountains and other southern parts of the country. The exceptions to this are the Sakha, herders and hunters who live in the Lena River Basin in eastern Siberia. They speak a language called Yakut, which is similar to Turkish.

Around 12,000 years ago there was still a land bridge between Asia and North America, where the Bering Strait is now. Some Sakha migrated east and continued their nomadic existence in parts of what are now Canada and the United States. Some of the first Americans were from Russia!

▼ A Sakha teenager studies a model of a traditional Sakha dwelling in a museum in Yakutsk.

remember the communist period, when religion was discouraged by the state. Another possible legacy of the old regime is that an unusually large number of Russians—about 20 percent of the population—claim to have no religion at all.

The second-largest faith group is Islam, with 5.5 percent of the population, mainly in the Caucasus and southern Volga regions. About 2 percent of Russians follow a non-Orthodox form of Christianity; most are Roman Catholic. A tiny minority of Russians are Buddhists. They live in the southeastern regions near Mongolia and China.

In the 19th century, there were millions of Jews living in Russia. The Jewish population has suffered persecution for some 200 years, however. It was attacked by both the Tsarist and Communist governments, and also by German invaders during World War II. Most Russian Jews have now moved to North America or Israel. Only about 140,000 still live in Russia, which is about 0.1 percent of the population.

On Thick Ice

In view of the climate, it is not surprising that the favorite Russian sports are ice-skating and cross-country skiing. In the summer, swimming, walking, and fishing are popular activities. In many parts of the country there are few facilities for more organized events, such as soccer and basketball matches.

Interest in tennis has increased since the 1990s, when Russia began to produce a stream of top stars, including Yevgeny Kafelnikov, Marat Safin, and—most successful of all—Maria Sharapova, who became the first Russian to win a Wimbledon singles title in 2004.

▲ Russian children can play ice hockey in the street in winter—but only for a short time; it gets dark early.

LORD OF THE EAST

The largest Russian city on the Pacific Ocean is Vladivostok; its name roughly translates as "Lord of the East." Formerly on Chinese territory, a port was opened there by the Russians in 1859. The city quickly became important because it gave access to Russia's only major sea routes that did not pass potentially hostile foreign countries. Shipping to and from the main Baltic ports, St. Petersburg and Kaliningrad, meant having to sail near Germany, while vessels from Odessa on the Black Sea had to go through the Turkish-controlled Dardanelles and then through the Mediterranean Sea before reaching the Atlantic Ocean.

Vladivostok became even more important after the completion of the Trans-Siberian Railway. Today, Vladivostok is an important naval and fishing port. There is much heavy industry there—and heavy pollution to go with it.

▲ Ships line up at the wharfs along Vladivostok's Golden Horn Bay.

X Marks the Spot

RUSSIA DOES NOT HAVE A LONG HISTORY of democracy. For 350 years, the country was ruled by decree: The tsar simply announced laws without needing the approval of the people. When the tsar was removed in 1917, the first election in Russian history was held to create a new government. The communists did not win enough votes to take power, so they seized control by a revolution instead. Russia continued to be run by unelected rulers.

That all changed in 1991, when Russians voted for the country's first president. A new constitution soon made Russia a full democracy, and a period of great change began. Some people worry that changes have happened too quickly. Democracy has not been derailed yet, however, as many feared it might be.

◀ Russian soldiers wait in line to vote at a polling station in Valdivostok during the parliamentary elections in 1999.

A FEDERATION ACROSS THE WORLD

Organizing a country as vast as Russia into a democracy is a difficult job. The country is a federation. It is split up into units that take care of certain responsibilities, but are still controlled by the government in Moscow. There are 86 federal units. Moscow and St. Petersburg are self-governing. Twenty-one areas are self-governing republics with their own presidents. They are generally the homelands of ethnic groups, and include Sakha and Chechnya. There are 49 oblasts (provinces). Most oblasts are based around a major city. Seven of the more remote oblasts are krai (territories). Seven areas are okrugs (districts). They have more power than oblasts but less than republics.

▼ The Mir diamond mine spirals 2,000 feet into eastern Siberia. The mine was the first of its kind in Russia. It was opened in 1955 and closed in 2004.

Trading Partners

Russia exports almost three times as much as it imports. Being such a large country means that Russia trades with its many neighbors. However, most business is done with the large economies of Europe. For example, Russia sells natural gas to Germany and other northern European countries through a series of huge pipelines running across the western border. Russia has many important trading partners in southern and Central Asia, too.

Russia exports crude oil, minerals, metals, food, and chemicals. Imports include gasoline and other refined fuels and machinery.

Country	Percent Russia exports
Netherlands	12.3%
Italy	8.6%
Germany	8.4%
All others combined	70.7%

Country	Percent Russia imports
Germany	13.9%
China	9.7%
Ukraine	7.0%
All others combined	69.4%

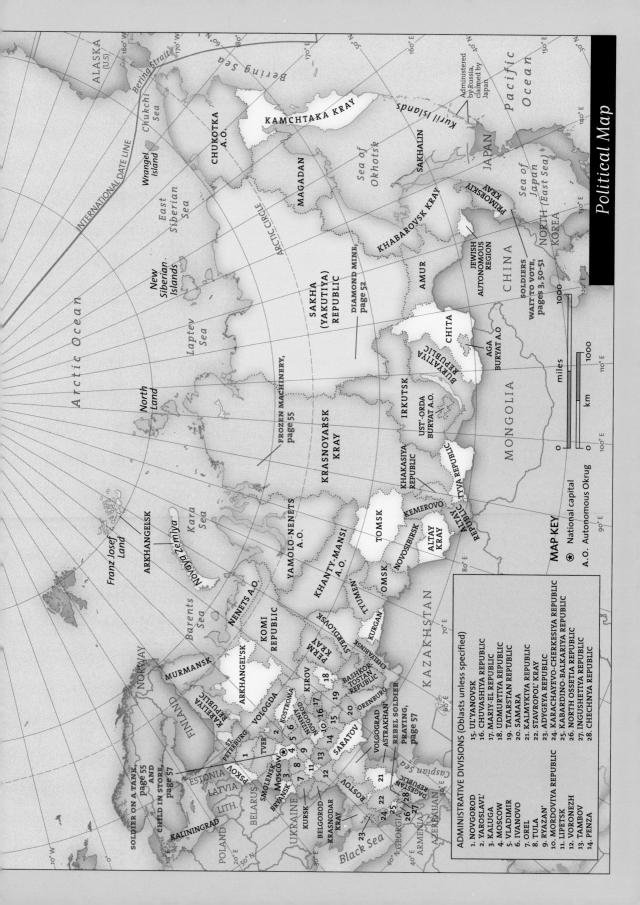

Political Map

ALASKA (U.S)

Bering Strait

Bering Sea

Chukchi Sea

Wrangel Island

INTERNATIONAL DATE LINE

CHUKOTKA A.O.

KAMCHTAKA KRAY

East Siberian Sea

New Siberian Islands

ARCTIC CIRCLE

MAGADAN

Sea of Okhotsk

SAKHALIN

Kuril Islands

Administered by Russia, claimed by Japan

JAPAN

Pacific Ocean

Arctic Ocean

North Land

FROZEN MACHINERY, page 55

SAKHA (YAKUTIYA) REPUBLIC

DIAMOND MINE, page 52

KHABAROVSK KRAY

AMUR

JEWISH AUTONOMOUS REGION

PRIMORSKIY KRAY

Sea of Japan (East Sea)

NORTH KOREA

CHINA

SOLDIERS WAIT TO VOTE, pages 3, 50-51

Franz Josef Land

Barents Sea

Novaya Zemlya

Kara Sea

Laptev Sea

KRASNOYARSK KRAY

CHITA

AGA BURYAT A.O.

BURYATIYA REPUBLIC

IRKUTSK

UST'-ORDA BURYAT A.O.

TYVA REPUBLIC

MONGOLIA

ARKHANGEL'SK

NENETS A.O.

KOMI REPUBLIC

YAMOLO-NENETS A.O.

KHANTY-MANSI A.O.

TOMSK

KEMEROVO

NOVOSIBIRSK

KHAKASIYA REPUBLIC

ALTAY KRAY

ALTAY REPUBLIC

80° E

MURMANSK

NORWAY

FINLAND

KARELIYA REPUBLIC

ARKHANGEL'SK

VOLOGDA

PERM KRAY

SVERDLOVSK

TYUMEN'

OMSK

KURGAN

CHELYABINSK

70° E

KAZAKHSTAN

MAP KEY

⊛ National capital

A.O. Autonomous Okrug

miles

km

1000

1000

ESTONIA

LATVIA

LITH.

KALININGRAD

POLAND

BELARUS

PSKOV

ST. PETERBURG

KIROV

BASHKOR-TOSTAN REPUBLIC

18

19

17

16

20

15

ORENBURG

10

6

KOSTROMA

NIZHNIY NOVGOROD

1

2

5

4

9

13

14

SARATOV

VOLGOGRAD

21

ASTRAKHAN

REBEL SOLDIER PRAYING, page 57

UKRAINE

SMOLENSK

Moscow ⊛

3

7

8

11

12

BRYANSK

KURSK

BELGOROD

KRASNODAR KRAY

ROSTOV

22

24

25

23

26

27

28

N. GEORGIA

ARMENIA

AZERBAIJAN

DAGESTAN REPUBLIC

Caspian Sea

Black Sea

40° E

50° N

60° E

SOLDIER ON A TANK, page 55 AND CHILD IN STORE, page 57

Hidden Treasures

Russia's economy is based on its vast supply of natural resources. Russia is the world's largest producer of natural gas, and the third-largest producer of crude oil. It has large supplies of coal and iron ore, and some of the world's richest deposits of gold, copper, nickel, and aluminum. The country has the world's largest forests, which produce a whole range of wood and paper products, and a huge "bread basket" where immense expanses of farmland grow wheat and corn.

Such resources should make Russia a very rich country, but it has two major problems. One is that much of its natural wealth lies in remote regions east

HOW THE GOVERNMENT WORKS

Russia's head of state is the president. He or she is elected by all the people and serves a maximum of two four-year terms. The president appoints the prime minister, cabinet ministers, and key judges. The Russian parliament has two chambers. The lower house—the State Duma—has 450 elected members. The upper house—the Federation Council—is composed of appointed senators. These legislators are appointed by regional governments. Two senators are sent from each of the federation's provinces, territories, and republics. Judges are appointed to the Supreme Court by the president and approved by the Federation Council.

GOVERNMENT		
EXECUTIVE	LEGISLATIVE	JUDICIARY
PRESIDENT	FEDERATION COUNCIL (172 MEMBERS)	SUPREME COURT
MINISTERS AND DIRECTORS	STATE DUMA (450 MEMBERS)	PROVINCIAL COURTS

THE SHOCK OF THE NEW

When Boris Yeltsin became the first president of Russia in 1991, he immediately set about transforming it into a Western-style free market economy. Not everyone supported his changes, which created much upheaval. However, Yeltsin was a powerful opponent. When communists tried to take over the country in 1991, he had them all thrown into prison. In 1993, when the parliament opposed his latest proposals, Yeltsin sent tanks to shell the parliament building. Nevertheless, Yeltsin was popular and was reelected in 1996.

Yeltsin was an alcoholic. Toward the end of his presidency, he often appeared drunk in public. He resigned as president on New

▲ A tank stands in front of the burning parliament building in Moscow during the 1993 crisis.

Year's Eve 1999, and made his deputy, Vladimir Putin, president. Yeltsin died in April 2007, and Putin remains Russia's leader.

of the Urals, while most of the population lives west of the mountains. The other difficulty is that, even now that Russia is a democracy, its political and economic systems are not very good at making full use of all of its opportunities.

▼ A thick layer of ice covers the machinery on an oil platform in western Siberia.

Government Sale

Under communism, the government owned all of Russia's industry. When Russia became a democracy, its new leaders sold the factories and mines to private companies. They hoped that the new owners would be able to update industry and encourage trade with foreign countries.

INDUSTRY MAP

This map shows the location of Russia's industrial centers. Most coal comes from the Lena River region in eastern Siberia. The largest oil and gas reserves are in the icy northwest of Siberia. Other mines are dotted across the country. Most iron ore comes from the Kursk Magnetic Anomaly, south of Moscow. This is a deposit of magnetic iron that is so immense that it stops compasses from working properly.

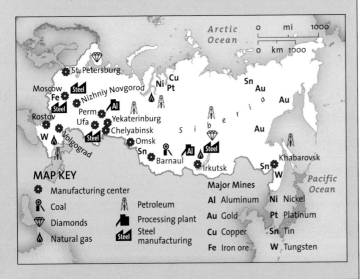

Arctic Ocean

0   mi   1000
0   km   1000

St. Petersburg
Moscow   **Steel**   Ni   Cu
Fe   Nizhniy Novgorod   Pt   Sn   Au
Steel   Perm   Al   Au
Rostov   Ufa   Yekaterinburg
W   Chelyabinsk   S   i   b   e   r   i   a   Au
Volgograd   Steel   Omsk
Sn   Al   Steel
Barnaul   Khabarovsk
Irkutsk   Sn
W   Pacific Ocean

MAP KEY

✿ Manufacturing center		**Major Mines**
🏹 Coal	🛢 Petroleum	**Al** Aluminum **Ni** Nickel
💎 Diamonds	🏭 Processing plant	**Au** Gold **Pt** Platinum
△ Natural gas	**Steel** Steel manufacturing	**Cu** Copper **Sn** Tin
		Fe Iron ore **W** Tungsten

▶ Russian *matryoshka* dolls traditionally contain a series of female dolls nested inside themselves. However, a doll of Russia's past and present leaders is now a popular tourist souvenir. From left to right: Putin, Yeltsin, and Gorbachev.

Although the sale made a small number of people fabulously wealthy, the Russian economy as a whole did not benefit.

Slow Start

In 2000, President Vladimir Putin warned that it would take Russia another 15 years to become even as wealthy as Portugal, one of the poorest members of the European Union (EU). Russian industry is old, slow, and sometimes unsafe. The steppes can grow enough crops to feed the people, but farming methods are also often inefficient. The average Russian worker produces only one-tenth of what a worker produces in the United States—and earns only one-tenth of an average American wage.

WAR AT HOME

▲ A Chechen rebel prays on the outskirts of Grozny during the First Chechen War.

Chechnya is a Russian republic in the Caucasus Mountains. One-third of its one million population is Muslin:. In 1994, Chechnya tried to gain independence from Russia. Moscow strongly opposed any move to split the federation, and sent in troops. That sparked the First Chechen War, a two-year conflict in which at least 50,000 people, mainly civilians, were killed. Russia called a ceasefire in 1996. However, Chechen fighters launched attacks on the neighboring republic of Dagestan. Chechen rebels were also behind terrorist attacks on Russian cities. Russian forces again moved into Chechnya and attacked the capital, Grozny—this was the Second Chechen War (1999–2000). Chechnya remains one of Russia's biggest problems. The independence movement has become a radical organization that wants to establish an Islamic government. Political unrest has now spread throughout the region.

However, the future looks bright. Russia supplies one-quarter of western Europe's gas. Its trawlers catch one-third of the world's canned fish and one-quarter of all fresh and frozen fish. Russian forests make a lot of the world's cardboard. The money made from selling these products is slowly making the lives of Russians better. Although it has a long way to go, Russia is on course to be one of the richest nations on Earth.

▼ A child wrapped up for winter weather looks at luxury goods in a Moscow store.

Add a Little Extra to Your Country Report!

I f you are assigned to write a report about Russia, you'll want to include basic information about the country, of course. The Fast Facts chart on page 8 will give you a good start. The rest of the book will providew the details you need to create a full and up-to-date paper or PowerPoint presentation. But what can you do to make your report more fun than anyone else's? If you use your imagination and dig a bit deeper into some of the topics introduced in this book, you're sure to come up with information that will make your report unique!

>Flag

Perhaps you could explain the history of Russia's flag, and the meanings of its colors. Go to **www.crwflags.com/fotw/flags** for more information.

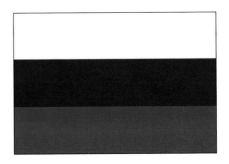

>National Anthem

How about downloading Russia's national anthem, and playing it for your class? At **www.nationalanthems.info** you'll find what you need, including the words to the anthem, plus sheet music for it. Simply pick "R" and then "Russia" from the list on the left-hand side of the screen, and you're on your way.

>Time Difference

If you want to understand the time difference between Russia and where you are, this Web site can help: **www.worldtimeserver.com**. Just pick "Russia" from the list on the left. If you called someone in Russia right now, would you wake them up from their sleep?

>Currency

Another Web site will convert your money into rubles, the currency used in Russia. You'll want to know how much money to bring if you're ever lucky enough to travel to Russia: **www.xe.com/ucc**.

>Weather

Why not check the current weather in Russia? It's easy—go to **www.weather.com** to find out if it's sunny or cloudy, warm or cold in Russia right now! Pick "World" from the headings at the top of the page. Then search for Russia. Click on any city. Be sure to click on the tabs below the weather report for Sunrise/Sunset information, Weather Watch, and Business Travel Outlook, too. Scroll down the page for the 36-hour Forecast and a satellite weather map. Compare your weather to the weather in the Russian city you chose. Is this a good season, weather-wise, for a person to travel to Russia?

>Miscellaneous

Still want more information? Simply go to National Geographic's World Atlas for Young Explorers at **http://www.nationalgeographic.com/kids-world-atlas/**. It will help you find maps, photos, music, games, and other features that you can use to jazz up your report.

Glossary

Climate the average weather of a certain place at different times of year.

Cold War a period of more than 30 years in which the communist world, led by the Soviet Union, and the free world, led by the United States, competed for power.

Communism a system of government where a single political party rules a country with the job of ensuring that wealth is shared equally among all the people in the country. Russia became the world's first communist state in 1917.

Conifer a tree that produces cones instead of flowers. Many conifers also have needles instead of leaves.

Culture a collection of beliefs, traditions, and styles that belongs to people living in a certain part of the world.

Democracy a country that is ruled by a government chosen by all its people through elections.

Economy the system by which a country creates wealth through making and trading in products.

Empire territories located in several parts of the world that are controlled by a single nation.

Ethnic group a section of a country's population with members that share a common ancestry or background.

Exile when someone is forced to leave their home country and live abroad.

Exported transported and sold outside the country of origin.

Gulag the system of Soviet prison camps, which were often in remote places.

Habitat a part of the environment that is suitable for certain plants and animals.

Illegal against the law.

Imported brought into the country from abroad.

Inhabited lived in by people.

Missionary a person who travels to a foreign country to spread a religion.

Natural resources naturally occurring materials and substances that can be collected and sold. Natural resources include oil, metals, or lumber.

Nomadic a person who moves from place to place rather than living in one place.

Pact a promise made by two people or countries to cooperate with each other.

Peninsula a narrow piece of land that is surrounded by water on three sides. The word means "almost island" in Latin.

Radical a person or organization that wants to make big changes to a country very quickly.

Revolutionary a person who wants revolution, the violent removal of a country's government.

Soviet Union a large empire of communist states that existed between 1922 and 1991. As well as Russia, the union included many other countries, such as Ukraine, and Armenia, which are now independent from each other.

Species a type of organism; animals or plants in the same species look similar and can only breed successfully among themselves.

Tsar a Russian emperor.

Bibliography

Corona, Laurel. *The Russian Federation*. San Diego, CA: Lucent Books, 2001.

Márquez, Herón. *Russia in Pictures*. Minneapolis, MN: Lerner Publications, 2004.

Matthews, John R. *The Rise and Fall of the Soviet Union*. San Diego, CA: Lucent Books, 2000.

http://kremlin.ru/eng/ (official Web site of the Kremlin, the Russian government building)

http://news.bbc.co.uk/1/hi/world/europe/country_profiles/1102275.stm (general information)

Further Information

NATIONAL GEOGRAPHIC Articles

Meier, Andrew. "Bitter Days for Chechnya." NATIONAL GEOGRAPHIC (July 2005): 78–89

Web sites to explore

More fast facts about Russia, from the CIA (Central Intelligence Agency): https://www.cia.gov/library/publications/the-world-factbook/geos/rs.html

How has Russia changed since Soviet times? This Web site has many photographs from the communist era. Other parts of the site contain information about the history of the Soviet union: http://www.marxists.org/history/ussr/art/photography/index.htm

Take a look at one of Russia's most beautiful cities—St. Petersburg. This Web site contains some stunning panoramas and a lot more pictures and information about the city: http://www.saint-petersburg.com/panoramas/index.asp

See, hear

There are many ways to get a taste of life in Russia, such as movies, music, magazines, or TV shows. You might be able to locate these:

Peter and the Wolf (1936) An enchanting ballet composed for children by Russian composer Sergei Prokofiev. The characters in the story, a boy, his grandfather, birds, hunters, and of course the wolf, are all represented by different melodies played on certain instruments.

The Moscow Times Find out what is happening in Russia today by reading the *Moscow Times*, Russia's main daily newspaper written in English: http://www.themoscowtimes.com/indexes/01.html

Voice of Russia Find out how Russians see themselves and the rest of the world by listening to the Voice of Russia, the country's foreign radio service. The radio broadcasts in English throughout the day and there are podcasts to download: http://www.ruvr.ru/index.php?lng=eng

Russia Today Watch videos of Russian news stories reported in English from the state news service: http://www.russiatoday.ru/

Index

Credits

Picture Credits

Front Cover – Spine: Atanas.dk/Shutterstock; Top: Sisse Brimberg/NGIC; Low Far Left: Marc Moritsch/NGIC; Low Left: Sergei Remezov/Reuters/Corbis; Low Right: Buddy Mays/Corbis; Low Far Right: Steve Raymer/NGIC.

Interior – Corbis: Bettmann: 35 up; Igor Bulmistrov/ITAR-T: 13 lo; Itar-Tass Pool/epa: 3 right, 50-51; Jacques/Langevin/Sygma: 2 left, 6-7; Wolfgang Kaehler: 49 lo; Gail Mooney: 30 lo; Reuters: 11 lo, 56 lo; Michel Setboun 29 up; Peter Turnley: 55 up, 57 up; NGIC: James P. Blair: 15 lo, 46 lo; Ira Block: 44 up; James P. Blair: 15 lo, 46 lo; Sisse Brimberg: 2-3, 10 lo, 24-25, 26 up; Jodi Cobb: 57 lo; Dean Conger: 20 up, 44lo, 47up, 48 lo, 49 up; Bruce Dale: 34 lo; Dick Durrance II: 31 up; Natalie B. Fobes: 21 lo; Sarah Leen: 11 up, 15 up, 20 lo, 23 center, 38 up; Gerd Ludwig: 55 lo; Marc Moritsch: 2 right, 16-17; Michael Nichols: 21 up; Richard Nowitz: 29 lo, 42 lo, 45 center; Randy Olson: 22 up; Steve Raymer: TP, 3 left, 5 up, 28 lo, 32 lo, 34 up, 35 lo, 36-37, 40 lo, 46 up; Norbert Rosing: 22 lo; Marina Sterizel: 42 up, 43 lo; Roy Toft: 19 center; Priit Vesilind: 12 up, 14 up; Cary Wolinsky: 30 up, 33 up, 52 lo; Shutterstock: Alexey Gostev: 59 up.

Text copyright © 2008 National Geographic Society
Published by the National Geographic Society.
All rights reserved. Reproduction of the whole or any part of the contents without written permission from the National Geographic Society is strictly prohibited.

For information about special discounts for bulk purchases, contact National Geographic Special Sales: ngspecsales@ngs.org
For rights or permissions inquiries, please contact National Geographic Books Subsidiary Rights: ngbookrights@ngs.org

For more information, please call 1-800-NGS-LINE (647-5463) or write to the following address:

NATIONAL GEOGRAPHIC SOCIETY
1145 17th Street N.W.
Washington, D.C. 20036-4688 U.S.A.

Visit us online at www.nationalgeographic.com/books

Library of Congress Cataloging-in-Publication Data available on request
ISBN: 978-1-4263-0259-6

Printed in the United States of America

Series design by Jim Hiscott.
The body text is set in Avenir; Knockout.
The display text is set in Matrix Script.

Front Cover—Top: Pedestrians in the snow in front of St. Basil's Cathedral in Red Square, Moscow; Low Left: Siberian tiger; Low Far Left: Cosmonauts with a Soyuz landing module; Low Right: Houses on the Volga River; Low Far Right: Dancers of the Mariinsky Ballet rehearse in St. Petersburg.

Page 1—T-shirts on sale in Moscow reflect Russia's communist past and the increased western influence on its economy. Icon image on spine, Contents page, and throughout: Russian dolls

Produced through the worldwide resources of the National Geographic Society

John M. Fahey, Jr., *President and Chief Executive Officer*; Gilbert M. Grosvenor, *Chairman of the Board*; Tim T. Kelly, *President, Global Media Group*; Nina D. Hoffman, *Executive Vice President, President of Book Publishing Group*

National Geographic Staff for this Book

Nancy Laties Feresten, *Vice President, Editor-in-Chief of Children's Books*
Bea Jackson, *Director of Design and Illustration*
Jim Hiscott, *Art Director*
Priyanka Lamichhane, *Project Editor*
Lori Epstein, *Illustrations Editor*
Stacy Gold, Nadia Hughes, *Illustrations Research Editors*
R. Gary Colbert, *Production Director*
Lewis R. Bassford, *Production Manager*
Maryclare Tracy, Nicole Elliott, *Manufacturing Managers*
Maps, *Mapping Specialists, Ltd.*

Brown Reference Group plc. Staff for this Book

Volume Editor: Tom Jackson
Designer: Dave Allen
Picture Manager: Clare Newman
Maps: Martin Darlinson
Artwork: Darren Awuah
Index: Kay Ollerenshaw
Senior Managing Editor: Tim Cooke
Design Manager: Sarah Williams
Children's Publisher: Anne O'Daly
Editorial Director: Lindsey Lowe

About the Author

HENRY RUSSELL is a British author and broadcaster. After graduating from Oxford University, he traveled widely, studying the business and social cultures of major European nations. He writes extensively for magazines, periodicals, and encyclopedias; this is his 15th book.

About the Consultants

LAURIE BERNSTEIN is an associate professor of history and director of women's studies at Rutgers University in Camden, New Jersey. She is the author of *Sonia's Daughters: Prostitutes and Their Regulation in Imperial Russia* (1995) and several articles on adoption in the Soviet Union, as well as the editor of Mary L. Leder's *My Life in Stalinist Russia: An American Woman Looks Back* (2001). Dr. Bernstein has spent lengthy periods of time in Russia both before and after the fall of communism.

ILYA UTEKHIN is head of the Department of Anthropology at the European University in St. Petersburg and lecturer in Semiotics and Communication at St. Petersburg State University. His best-known contribution to Russian and Soviet studies are a book and a multimedia web-museum dedicated to urban housing and everyday life in the USSR. He also works in visual anthropology.

Time Line of Russian History

A.D.

600s The first permanent settlements are founded on the Volga River by Scandinavian settlers.

882 Kiev and Novgorod are united as the state of Kievan Rus.

988 Vladimir I converts to Orthodox Christianity and makes Eastern Orthodoxy the official religion.

1147 Moscow is founded as a defensive outpost.

1236 Mongols, also known as Tatars, invade southern Russia, destroying many cities, interrupting trade with the Byzantine Empire, and imposing heavy taxes on the Russians.

1480 Ivan III frees Russia from Tatar control. Moscow becomes the most powerful Russian city.

1500

1547 Russia is the largest European state and Ivan IV, also known as Ivan the Terrible, is crowned its first tsar.

1556 Ivan IV conquers the Tatar khanates of Kazan and Astrakhan to establish Russian rule over lower and middle Volga.

1581 Ivan IV contracts Cossack mercenaries to expand Russian influence into Siberia and gain access to the Pacific.

1600

1613 A national council elects Mikhail Romanov tsar, beginning 300 years of Romanov rule of Russia.

1649 Ivan III establishes the institution of serfdom, a system by which peasant families are tied to wealthy estates.

1682 Peter the Great comes to the throne. He will introduce far-reaching reforms, modernizing Russia to become more like its European neighbors.

1700

1703 Peter the Great orders the construction of St. Petersburg as Russia's new capital.

1772 Russia begins a period of expansion that will add the Crimea to its territory as well as parts of Poland, Ukraine, Belarus, Moldova, and Georgia.

1796 Catherine the Great's collection of 3,000 paintings is installed in the Hermitage Palace, which will provide the basis for the Hermitage Museum.

1800

1812 Napoleon I invades Russia and marches on Moscow; Muscovites abandon the city, forcing Napoleon to retreat. Bitter winter temperatures and starvation kill four-fifths of Napoleon's troops.

1825 The Decembrist Revolution calls for democratic reforms; Nicholas I crushes the protests and becomes tsar.

1857 After four years of fighting, Russia is defeated in the Crimean War by France and its British, Ottoman, and Sardinian allies over control of the Middle East.

1861 Alexander II issues the Emancipation Edict that ends serfdom and allows serfs to move to rapidly industrializing cities.